The Tarantula Scientist

W9-BXZ-357

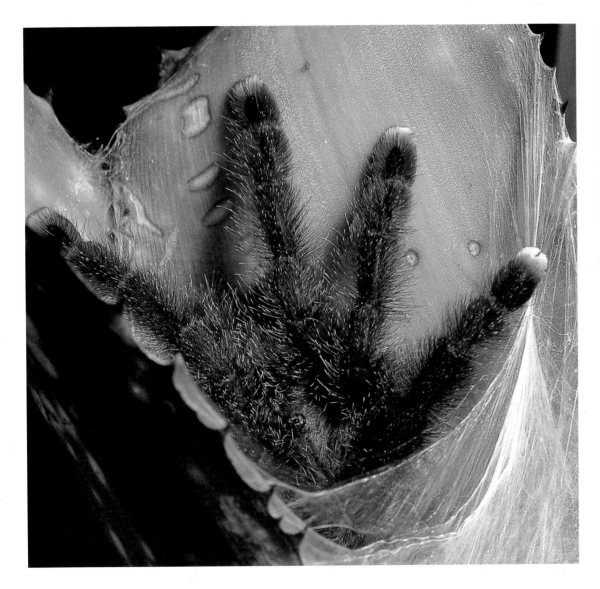

The Tarantula Scientist

TEXT BY **Sy Montgomery**

PHOTOGRAPHS BY **Nic Bishop**

Houghton Mifflin Company

Boston

To Clarabelle,
a great tarantula
—S.M.

For Bill,
Kiwi colleague
—N.B.

Text copyright © 2004 by Sy Montgomery
Photographs copyright © 2004 by Nic Bishop

All rights reserved. For information about permission to reproduce
selections from this book, write to Permissions, Houghton Mifflin
Company, 215 Park Avenue South, New York, New York 10003.

www.hmhbooks.com

Book design by Lisa Diercks
The text of this book is set in Ottomat Book.

Library of Congress Cataloging-in-Publication Control Number
2003020125

ISBN-13: 978-0-618-14799-1 (hardcover)
ISBN-13: 978-0-618-91577-4 (paperback)

HALF TITLE, LEFT PHOTOGRAPH: A pinktoe rests in its retreat inside a
bromeliad plant. HALF TITLE, RIGHT PHOTOGRAPH: Sam, the tarantula
scientist. PHOTOGRAPH FACING TITLE PAGE: Venom droplets hang from
the fangs of a Brazilian black tarantula. Although people are often
fearful of tarantulas, these spiders usually bite only in self-defense.

Printed in Mexico
RDT 18 17 16 15 14
4500427918

UNITED STATES OF AMERICA

GULF OF
MEXICO

BAHAMA
ISLANDS

Tropic of Cancer

CUBA

TURKS &
CAICOS
ISLANDS

DOM

MEXICO

BELIZE

JAMAICA

HAITI

CARIBBEAN SEA

HONDURAS

GUATEMALA

EL
SALVADOR

NICARAGUA

PANAMA

COSTA
RICA

PACIFIC

OCEAN

COLOMBIA

ECUADOR

GALÁPAGOS
ISLANDS

PERU

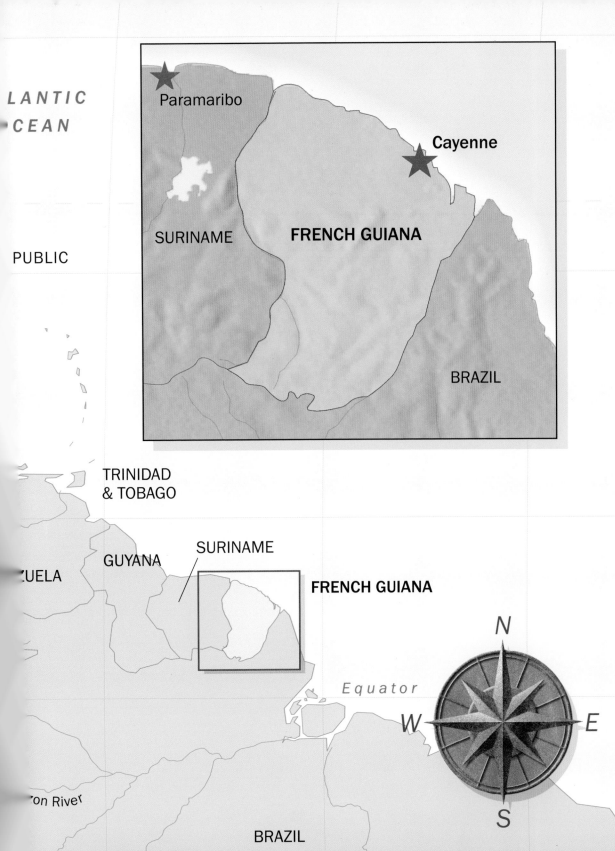

ATLANTIC OCEAN

Paramaribo

Cayenne

SURINAME

FRENCH GUIANA

BRAZIL

PUBLIC

TRINIDAD
& TOBAGO

GUYANA

SURINAME

FRENCH GUIANA

VENEZUELA

Equator

N

W   E

S

BRAZIL

...on River

Just north of the equator, French
Guiana's steamy rainforests are home
to about a dozen species of tarantulas.

Queen of the Jungle

Sam Marshall is lying on his belly in the rainforest, his freckled face just inches from a fist-sized hole in the dirt. He turns on his headlamp. He gently pokes a twig into the tunnel and wiggles it. "Come out!" he says into the hole. "I want to meet you!"

Normally, it's not a great idea to poke sticks into burrows in the jungle—especially if you don't know who lives there. Snakes, for instance, don't appreciate it. In this particular rainforest, the most common snake is the fer-de-lance. The name means "spearhead" in French, which suggests you'd better not bother one.

"AVERTISSEMENT!" (French for "WARNING!") reads the rough-hewn sign at the head of the jungle trail to Trésor Réserve. The sign warns visitors to beware of snakes—and, while they're at it, to watch out for spiders, wasps, biting ants, bees, wild pigs, slippery trails, roots poking up from the ground, and branches falling down from the trees.

But Sam knows this forest well. He knows exactly what he's doing. Sam is a spider scientist, or arachnologist (pronounced "ar-rack-NAWL-o-gist"). His specialty? The biggest, hairiest, and, some would say, scariest group of spiders on earth: tarantulas. That's why he's come all the way from Hiram, Ohio, to French Guiana in South America.

FACING PAGE: Sam uses a "fishing stick" to trick a Goliath birdeater out of its burrow.

Just north of the equator, French Guiana is home to only 150,000 people. It's about the size of Indiana. But for its size, this is probably the tarantula capital of the world. Perhaps a dozen species of tarantulas live here, including some of the most spectacular.

So far, Sam has caught only a glimpse of hairy legs in the hole. But he knows who's in there: a Goliath birdeater tarantula, the largest species of spider on the planet.

How big might that be? Big enough that with outstretched legs, this spider could cover your whole face. A large one could weigh as much as five mice. This tarantula is a Goliath for sure!

Sam isn't frightened at all. "C'mon, sweetie!" he calls down the hole. Sam is trying to lure the spider out. Normally tarantulas spend the day waiting in their silk-lined retreats. They come out at night to sit in front of the burrow. There they wait for prey. But by wiggling the stick as if it were a juicy worm or a scuttling cockroach—a meal the Goliath birdeater, despite its name, would probably prefer to a bird—Sam hopes to coax her out into daylight.

There! Sam feels her grab the twig with the pair of food-handling feet, called pedipalps, next to the front of her head. "She's pretty strong," he says. He knows she's a female because he can already see how big she is. Females are bigger than males and live much longer.

He wiggles the stick some more. He thinks she'll come out if the "prey" seems to be trying to get away. And he's right: "Here she comes," he announces.

She *thunders* out of the hole! Her eight walking feet, each tipped with two claws called tarsi, patter loudly on the dead leaves on the forest floor. "These tarantulas are the jaguars of the leaf litter," Sam says. And it's true—to the frogs and worms and insects who live here, this tarantula must be an awesome predator.

Even for a big mammal like a human, the sight of a Goliath birdeater tarantula rushing out of her burrow takes your breath away. She's not even full grown, but her head is the size of a fifty-cent piece. Her abdomen is bigger than a quarter. All of her body, including each of the seven segments of her eight strong, long legs, is covered with rich, deep reddish brown hairs, some of them half an inch long.

When she races out, she looks as if she might rush up Sam's arm—maybe onto his face! And if she does, will she bite him? Would he die?

The giant tarantula stops abruptly, just four inches past the mouth of her burrow. Even though her eight eyes are almost blind, her other senses—which include chemical senses humans can only dream of—tell her the bad news: No meal here. And then, quite reasonably, she backs down partway into her burrow.

Sam ties a bit of bright pink plastic tape to a nearby tree to help him find the burrow again later. He gets up to leave, to find more spiders. The tarantula doesn't vanish down the hole; she waits calmly, still near the mouth of her burrow. Three adult humans—Sam and two companions—thud past her. To her fine-tuned sense of touch, the vibrations must shake the very earth. Surely she realizes that nearly five hundred pounds' worth of monsters are clomping around just inches from her home!

"Yeah, but why should she care?" Sam says. "She's Queen of the Jungle!"

The largest spider on earth, the Goliath birdeater tarantula guards its burrow entrance.

Sam is thrilled every time he sees a Goliath birdeater tarantula. He is in awe of this giant spider. "They really are, at the level of the forest floor, the masters," he says.

But he's never been frightened of them.

He has handled hundreds of tarantulas and worked with them thousands of times. He's never been bitten—not once. "They don't have a bloodlust to bite people," Sam says. "The last thing they want to do is bite you! They'd rather be left alone. They are just really interesting, beautiful animals, not horrible creatures."

In fact, not one single person has ever died as a result of a tarantula bite. Tarantulas don't attack people. They attack only what they want to eat, and, happily, tarantulas don't eat us. (People eat them, though. In the jungle, people roast them to burn the hairs off before eating them—and sometimes use the cooked tarantulas' leftover fangs to pick their own teeth afterward.)

For most tarantulas, biting is a defense they'd rather not use at all. They'd rather hide. If that doesn't work, some tarantulas use a defense more effective than fangs or venom: their hairs!

How can tarantulas use hair to protect themselves? Sam explains: When irritated, most New World tarantulas (those from North and South America) will use their rear pair of legs to kick hairs off their back end. Each hair is covered with tiny barbs like a porcupine quill but is light enough to float on air currents.

Tarantulas don't go hunting for prey. They wait for something tasty, like this cockroach, to walk within reach, then pounce.

Sam has had a few "hairy" experiences himself. He knows firsthand that these barbed hairs can get into the folds of skin in your neck, between your fingers, into your eyes, up your nose. The result? Itching and sneezing that make a smart predator leave the tarantula alone.

Though tarantulas are much less scary than you probably thought, they're far stranger than you might have imagined. In fact, *all* spiders are pretty amazing! They smell with their feet. They taste with special hairs on their feet and legs. They wear their skeleton on the outside instead of the inside. That's why their "skin" is called an exoskeleton, because *exo*—like exit—means "outside." Their exoskeleton isn't made of bone but of cuticle, the same stuff you peel off a cooked shrimp. Even tarantulas' hairs are not really hairs, but very fine cuticle.

Spiders seem like creatures from another planet. Their blood is clear, or sometimes pale blue or yellow. They periodically shed all their exoskeletal "skin"—and even the lining of the mouth, stomach, and lungs. Tarantulas do this while lying on their back with their feet in the air. They can regrow lost legs. Sometimes a tarantula will pull off its own injured leg—and then eat it (proving the old saying "You are what you eat")!

Look at a tarantula and you can clearly see the astonishing body plan of all spiders. Their body parts seem to be in all the wrong places, or doing the wrong things, or too numerous, or too few. The head is covered with eyes (eight), fangs (two), and legs (eight). The stomach, too, is in the head. (After all, spiders have just two big body parts, the head and the abdomen.) Some spiders, including most common house spiders, digest their food BEFORE they eat it. First the spider bites and paralyzes the prey with venom. Then it pumps fluid from its stomach into the victim. In a few moments, the inside of the prey has turned to liquid. Yum! The spider slurps out the juice and then tosses the skin away like an empty juice box. Some spiders, though, do things differently: tarantulas, for instance, grind up their food with teeth behind their fangs.

Spiders, with their silk and strength and grace, have abilities we'd like in our comic book heroes—like Spiderman. But if spiders have their own heroes, they are probably tarantulas.

Tarantulas are superspiders, and not just because they're so big and strong and hairy. Most spiders live only a season or two. Some tarantulas can live thirty years. And tarantulas are among the world's most ancient groups of spiders. Sam considers them "sort of spider dinosaurs." Tarantulas have been around for more than 150 million years—and, unlike the dinosaurs, they're not extinct. They have a lot to teach us!

Yet, like our superheroes, these superspiders have many secrets. They are mystery animals. Scientists know very little about them. Sam is one of only four or five scientists who study tarantulas. "Tarantulas are understudied and underappreciated," says Sam.

Take the Goliath birdeater tarantula. Scientists don't have any idea how many there are. How do they select their burrows? Does each spider dig one, or

An adult female tarantula sheds her skin about once a year. First she spins a silk molting mat in the safety of her burrow. Then she rolls onto her back, wriggling and struggling for hours to squeeze off the old skin. Afterward, she lies exhausted while her new skin hardens and darkens.

does it take over a hole made by another animal? Do they live in spider neighborhoods, or just anywhere all over the forest? How fast do they grow? How long do they live in the wild? How much space do they need? Nobody knows.

So little is known about the Goliath birdeater that only twice have scientists seen one kill and eat anything in the wild. (Once, it was a big worm. Another time, a legless, wormlike amphibian called a caecilian.) "It's especially amazing considering that here you have the biggest of something in the world," Sam says, "and nobody knows anything about it!"

That's what Sam is doing here in the rainforest. "Basically," Sam says, "what I want to know is, what is life like for the world's largest spider?" It's work he continues back at his laboratory at Hiram College in Ohio. The mystery of tarantulas drew Sam to them in the first place. And the tarantulas, in turn, lured him to this rainforest and inspired him to become a scientist.

Many tarantulas are really quite beautiful, like this Martinique pinktoe (FACING PAGE) and Chilean rose hair (RIGHT).

When Is a Tarantula a Tarantula?

In Malaysia, they call them "earth tigers." In parts of Africa, "monkey spiders." But one thing tarantulas were never called was "tarantulas"—until European explorers made a mistake.

The big, hairy spiders we know as tarantulas aren't the "original" tarantulas. The name was first used for a two- to three-inch-long wolf spider from Mediterranean Europe. People thought this spider had a really nasty bite. (As it turns out, they wrongly blamed the big wolf spider for the bite of another, less showy spider, a relative of the black widow.) The bite was said to hurt so much that people who were bitten would dance around, trying to get rid of the venom. They called the dance the tarantella, named after the Italian town of Taranto. That's where the original tarantula got its name.

When European explorers went to the tropics and started finding giant, hairy, scary-looking spiders, they called them all tarantulas. Wrong again! Tropical tarantulas are very different spiders.

The tropical tarantulas and their relatives were on Earth long before the Mediterranean tarantula. Tropical tarantulas—a group of spiders scientists sometimes call hairy mygalomorphs—were among the planet's original spiders. They first appeared long, long ago when half the world was glommed together in two big supercontinents. The one the tarantulas lived on later broke up into South America, Australia, Africa, Antarctica, and part of Asia. Today, different kinds of tarantulas are found on all of these continents except Antarctica, plus parts of North America and Europe, too. Some live in trees. Some live in holes. And some even live in people's houses. Not all of them are giants. Some are smaller than the long-legged spiders who probably live in your basement. But all of them share certain features, just like family traits.

All of the tropical tarantulas are in what scientists call a family

A wolf spider carries her egg sac.

of spiders. Scientists are always sorting things into categories, the way you might sort your clothes: You might keep all your winter clothes in one closet, and in that closet you might keep all the pants in one section, and shirts in another. Within the shirt section, you might have all the flannel shirts grouped together, separate from the turtlenecks. And so on.

The biggest category for scientists is the kingdom. Spiders are in the animal kingdom. The animal kingdom itself is split into two major groups, depending on whether the animal has an internal skeleton or not. Those who don't are called invertebrates (*in* means "not"—as in "*in*accurate" or "*in*considerate"; *vertebrate* comes from the word for the backbone, or vertebrae, of the skeleton.)

The invertebrates are a big crowd of critters. Invertebrates include not only spiders, but also worms, crabs, jellyfish, all the insects from beetles to butterflies—and quite a few others. In fact, most animals on Earth aren't vertebrates, like whales and people, snakes and birds. More than 90 percent of all animals on Earth are little, spineless invertebrates! So it's a good thing that within the invertebrates scientists make more categories.

After all, spiders aren't much like worms or jellyfish. They're not

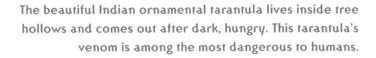
The beautiful Indian ornamental tarantula lives inside tree hollows and comes out after dark, hungry. This tarantula's venom is among the most dangerous to humans.

even insects. All insects have three major body parts and six legs. But count up spider parts and you'll see how different they are: Like mites, scorpions, ticks, and daddy longlegs (also called harvestmen), all spiders have two main body parts and eight legs. They are all arachnids ("uh-RACK-nids"), a word that comes from the Greek word for spider. Spiders are their own group within the arachnids. All spiders have venom (though most of the time the venom can't hurt people), and all spiders make silk.

Scientists further sort spiders into families. There are about sixty spider families in the world. One family is the jumping spiders. They come in different shapes and sizes, but all of them have two really big eyes in addition to all the small ones. Another family is the orb web spiders. They include the garden spiders who weave big, pretty webs. The Mediterranean spider is a species of wolf spider, a family of spiders who hunt their prey on foot rather than snare it in a web.

The tropical and subtropical tarantulas are all one family, the Theraphosidae. They're named for the Latin word for "small animal." (You'd think they might have named it "big spider" instead!) From here on in this book, we'll use the word *tarantula* as Sam does: to refer to members of the family Theraphosidae.

So what unites the family? Several features set them apart. Because tarantulas are such ancient spiders, two parts of their bodies are still kind of old-fashioned.

Tarantulas breathe using two pairs of "book lungs" (so called because they look like the pages

Apart from spiders, the arachnids include scorpions, vinegaroons (which can squirt acid "vinegar"), daddy longlegs (or harvestmen), ticks, and mites. All have eight legs (the animals are named in order of their size in the illustration).

of this book). Most spiders have one pair of book lungs, plus breathing tubes called tracheae, which deliver oxygen directly to different parts of the spider's body. The tracheae are a relatively new invention. Too bad tarantulas missed out! The breathing tubes help spiders conserve water. Book lungs lose a lot of water through evaporation. This can put a thirsty tarantula in big trouble. Spiders, unlike mammals, use blood pressure instead of muscles to straighten their legs. Since blood is mainly water, a tarantula who's thirsty may not be able to walk.

Another old-fashioned feature is the tarantula's fangs, which move only up and down. All other spiders' fangs move sideways. The "new-fangled" way allows spiders to bite faster and easier. They don't have to rear up and stab their victims with their fangs, as tarantulas do.

But the tarantula family is still doing just fine, thank you. There are 850 different kinds—small, medium, large, and (as in the Goliath birdeater) extra-large; hairy and extra-hairy; some with gorgeous stripes, some with red knees, some with bright orange bellies. Some come in purple and shiny blue!

Few other groups of spiders are so varied, successful, and widespread. They live almost everywhere that is warm enough: from the southwestern deserts of the United States to the rainforests of Australia. Even without the latest design in fangs, even with their old-fashioned book lungs, tarantulas have conquered much of the world.

Jumping spiders (this one is from Costa Rica) have the best eyesight of all spiders.

An up-close look at a Goliath birdeater (underside)

Eating and mating. Two pedipalps are used for handling food. Males also use them to store sperm for mating.

Venom delivery. Fangs are hollow and inject the prey with venom.

Hissing hairs. Pale bristles on the inside of the front legs make a warning hissing noise when rubbed together.

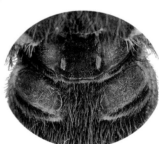

Breathing system. Four book lungs under the body absorb oxygen.

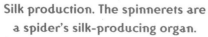

Silk production. The spinnerets are a spider's silk-producing organ.

Hair defense. Tiny irritating barbed hairs on the abdomen can be released to deter predators.

Science and Spiders

"**A**AHHHH!!!"

When you hear this sound coming from a tarantula scientist, you know something's really wrong.

The next noise from Sam's direction is equally disturbing. It's the sound of 230 pounds of arachnologist rolling down a rainforest slope.

"Sam?" calls out one of his helpers. "What's wrong?"

After a moment comes his matter-of-fact reply: "I found a wasp's nest."

Unfortunately, Sam found it by smacking his head into it. "I was so focused on looking for tarantulas I didn't see anything else," he explains. The nest was easy to miss. Only six inches long, it's the same brown color as the dead leaf to which it's attached. Now about 150 unhappy, black half-inch wasps are buzzing around it. Several of them stung Sam's face and neck. The fastest way to get away from them was to roll downhill.

Luckily, Sam is feeling fine in a few minutes—and eager to find more tarantulas. He has some medicine in his backpack for stings and bites. It's just one of the odd things a tarantula researcher needs to do science in the rainforest. Besides his heavy load of drinking

The tarantula hawk is a tarantula's worst enemy. These large wasps hunt tarantulas and paralyze them with a sting. The wasp lays an egg nearby, and when it hatches, the wasp grub feeds on the still-living tarantula.

water, which is very important in the 90-degree heat and 99 percent humidity, Sam is also carrying quite a bit of scientific equipment. Let's take a look at some of his supplies:

- plastic deli containers for potato salad (which will soon hold tarantulas instead)
- several rolls of plastic tape in different colors (for marking burrows)
- dozens of empty pill bottles ("Take two small tarantulas and call me in the morning . . .")
- some giant tweezers (for urging tarantulas into potato salad containers)
- a big kitchen knife (for digging burrows)
- a hoe (for chopping roots)

These may not sound like scientific supplies—but then, what Sam does for a living may not sound like your science class at school. When Sam was growing up, he couldn't imagine that science could be this exciting!

"I had no idea what it meant to be a scientist or a biologist," Sam admits. "I think my impression was the same as most people's: that science is a body of knowledge, that science is a big book of answers." Science, to him, was about memorizing a bunch of facts—not figuring out new ways to solve mysteries and make new discoveries.

"Science," as he understood it, didn't interest him at all.

What did interest him was animals. As a little boy he kept a lizard, gerbils, mice, and a rabbit. Then followed frogs, toads, salamanders, snakes, bugs—he would catch them all and then set up homes for them in tanks in his room.

He loved to watch them. "Animals are a whole different life form," Sam explains, "and I was drawn to things that are different. One of the most powerful ways to have interaction with animals is to actually care for them and feed them and work with them every day. I was so curious about how they lived and what they did."

When Sam was thirteen, his family visited New Mexico. They stopped at a park to visit a ranger friend of Sam's father. On his desk in a terrarium was a hairy spider. It was the first tarantula Sam ever saw.

His younger sister was scared. His baby brother was not impressed. But Sam was enchanted. "I was fascinated with it," he remembers. "It was small compared to these *Theraphosa,* but it looked huge to me." He had never seen a creature so different, so intriguing, so mysterious.

Soon, tarantulas joined his growing menagerie. When Sam went to college, he moved into his dorm room with ferrets, a hawk, a ball python, a monitor lizard, zebra finches—and a host of scorpions and tarantulas. (The dean of students at Bard College told him he had to move the scorpions to the biology department. But the others could stay in his room.) His roommate was pleased. It made their room a popular place for other students to visit.

But Sam didn't do well in school. He got bad grades even in biology. Until, that is, he had to do a special

Wasp nests hanging from leaves are a hazard you can bump into when searching for tarantulas.

project in his third year of college. He decided to do a scientific research project on his favorite animals—tarantulas.

He decided to compare desert tarantulas and rainforest tarantulas: Which ones were more energetic, and why? How did different temperatures affect the different species? He went to Arizona to catch desert tarantulas. He traveled all the way to Venezuela in South America to catch rainforest tarantulas. He captured about a dozen of each species and set up tanks for them at his college. The tarantulas were so happy and comfortable in Sam's tanks, some even had babies there.

Sam set up his own laboratory. He even designed special machines to measure how much oxygen each tarantula breathed, and at what rate, and at which temperature.

LEFT: A tarantula, like this PTERINOCHOLUS, will try to scare an attacker by rearing up to show its fangs.

FACING PAGE: The diversity of life in the rainforest gives Sam pause to wonder. A huge and ancient tree like the one he is resting on may harbor more types of ants, beetles, spiders, and other small creatures than the whole 260 acres of forest at the Barrow Field Station that Sam looks after in Ohio.

He found out that the rainforest species needed more oxygen and breathed faster than the desert tarantulas. But far more important was another discovery: Sam found out that he loved science almost as much as he loved tarantulas.

"I got so into this, and then I realized: I loved research! And I realized science really is a process. It's not the knowledge the process generates," Sam says. "Once I understood that anybody can do the process, it's very simple—scientific research is just a way of asking a question and answering it. That was the thing that totally changed my life."

Asking questions about tarantulas and answering them is just what Sam and his colleagues are doing, combing the rainforest slopes today. One very important question he's asking about Goliath birdeaters is, where do they live? It's well worth a few wasp stings to get the answer—and it's fun to find out.

"Let's divide and search for holes with big hairy legs in them," Sam suggests.

There are plenty of holes to search. Everyone seems to make holes in this red, shallow soil: snakes, armadillos, certain wasps, toads, lizards, tortoises, opossums. But the holes of Goliath birdeaters are easy to tell apart from the others. Shaped like the mouth of a cave, these two-inch holes are flat on the bottom and round on the top, and usually under a branch, root, or stone. They're almost always on a steep slope ("They like a room with a view," Sam says).

That makes for slippery going, if you're walking on slopes covered with slick wet leaves. The best way to hunt for the burrows, Sam says, is by walking uphill, because the holes seem to be pointing up at you. "And if you slip downhill," Sam advises, "you'll eventually crash into a tree and stop."

Sam believes the Goliaths tend to live in clumps. That's why this morning they've

ABOVE: Sam uses pink tape to tag a tree near a burrow.

RIGHT: Sam walks with a compass and reels out a
fifty-meter tape to mark out a study plot.

returned to the area where he found the Goliath bird-eater yesterday (whom he named "Rosie" because of the pink tape he used to mark the burrow.) Where there's one, there might be others.

He's right! Sure enough—past the vine that grows in twirls like a corkscrew, over the snaky roots of that big tree, around the squat, spiny palm comes the sound of a very happy tarantula scientist:

"Yay! Hairy Legs! It's a *Theraphosa!*"

He marks that burrow with bright pink tape, too.

And just twenty-seven slippery paces from *that* tarantula—over the rotting log, past the giant tree covered in vines, around the big rock—he finds another burrow. And just ten feet away, he finds yet another.

"Now we know what area to do the quadrant in," Sam says, pleased.

A quadrant is a sort of grid that scientists use to map out an area and measure its features or the ways animals use that area. There seem to be a lot of tarantulas in this spot. The question is, how many is a lot?

The answer depends on how big an area you're

Tiny poison dart frogs are common at the study site. Their colors warn predators that they are poisonous.

looking at. Six tarantulas might not seem like a lot of spiders if they were spread out all over French Guiana. But they would sure seem like a lot if they were all in your bed!

So Sam wants to find out how many tarantulas he can find in an area of a specific size. His quadrant is a square fifty meters by fifty meters (one meter is 39.37 inches). He marks off the square using a long tape measure and marks its boundaries with more brightly colored plastic tape tied to trees. He and his helpers will then carefully count every Goliath burrow within it.

How will he know if there are a lot or just a few? You guessed it: He needs to compare the number of burrows in this quadrant with the number he finds in other areas the same size. So he'll have to do several quadrants—and meet a lot more tarantulas. This way he'll begin to answer other important questions: Are Goliath birdeaters all over the forest? Or do they prefer very specific areas? What are those areas like? What do these tarantulas need?

For Sam, finding answers to questions in science sometimes means hours of experiments in his Hiram laboratory. Today it means climbing over giant fallen trees covered with orchids and mosses as he makes his measurements. It means long hikes through a wet, warm rainforest where even the sunlight glows green through the leaves. The rainforest is alive with strange voices: the thrumming of frogs and crickets, the screech of red and gold macaw parrots flying overhead, and the sound Sam likes best: the stuttered wolf whistle of the screaming piha. Sam calls it "the *Theraphosa* bird" because he tends to hear its call in areas where he finds the most Goliath birdeaters.

Sam never knows what he might find on a day in the rainforest. One day he might nearly stumble over a giant red-necked tortoise climbing out of its burrow. Another day he might catch a glimpse of a troop of howler monkeys in the trees. And every day he gets to learn more about tarantulas—the most beautiful, intriguing, and mysterious creatures he has ever known.

Secrets of the Burrow

"**S**trike! Strike! Strike! Backing up . . . strike!" Sam is lying in the dirt again, looking down into a tarantula burrow. Like a sportscaster, he's narrating what he sees: "Ooh, she's reared up, and not very pleased with me.

"It doesn't look like she wants to come out and play," he says, disappointed with the stubborn spider. But he can't blame her. A few minutes earlier, Sam had enticed her out with his "twizzle" stick. Once she figured out that that was a hoax, she wisely decided to stay in her burrow.

It's a nice place to stay, after all. "Tarantulas are tidy little homemakers," Sam explains. They don't use their burrows as bathrooms. When a tarantula feels the need, it carefully backs out of its burrow; then its droppings don't drop but spray—far away from the hole called home. And tarantulas probably don't use the burrow as a garbage disposal, either. In captivity, they almost always push the remains of their prey into a corner (which often turns out to be the water dish.)

This burrow is a fine example of the tarantula's neat habits. "She's a regular eight-legged

Martha Stewart!" Sam says. "It's not a messy, smelly hole. It's a nice hole, clean and dry inside, and lined with silk."

Though tarantulas don't weave webs with their silk, they use this amazing substance, which they pull out of their own bodies, in other fascinating ways. Look at this burrow: Like most occupied Goliath birdeater homes, it sports a little welcome mat of silk. The silk might help her sense when a prey item is coming—a visitor who would be welcome indeed! At night the tarantula sits there on the mat the way a person might spend an evening on the front porch, waiting for a pizza delivery.

But this tarantula isn't coming out. She's not going to fall for that twizzle-stick trick again—not right away, anyway. Sam decides to leave her alone for a bit to let her calm down.

After a few minutes, as he sits beside the burrow, a nine-inch nightcrawler comes squirming by. That gives Sam an idea. "If life gives you worms," Sam reasons, "make spider bait!" He plucks a loose thread from his

Tarantulas are tidy burrow makers. This red skeleton tarantula has a miniature garden of ferns and moss decorating the vaselike entrance to its burrow.

backpack and ties the worm to it. He ties the other end of the thread to a flexible twig. Now he's got a spider-fishing pole.

Sam pushes the baited twig down the burrow. He feels the Goliath grab it! But when Sam reels the stick back in, there is no spider on the end. And there's just half a worm.

Only now—having invested most of half an hour next to this burrow—does Sam decide to dig. He uses his carving knife very gently, because he doesn't want to hurt the spider. He uses the blade only to chop roots. "All right," he announces to the giant spider, "come out with your tarsi up!"

But while he's digging, he comes across another burrow that seems to connect to this one. "What have we here?" Sam asks. Exploring further, he soon discovers an entirely different spider! "Something new!" he says. "A very strange tarantula—an animal I haven't seen before! Short hair, grayish legs, red abdomen, and suspiciously leggy—almost like a species I know from Trinidad."

When Sam pulls out the "fishing stick" there is only half a worm left on it.

Sam digs deeper, now using his hoe. "Come back!" he cries as the spider scoots down its burrow. "We need you!"

With his other hand, he removes the lid from one of the pill bottles. When he reaches the bottom of the burrow, he covers the spider with the bottle and then closes the cap (which has breathing holes punched in it).

He examines his prize: "I have no idea what this is. It might not even be a tarantula. It's beautiful, though. It might be a wolf spider. But it's furry like a tarantula and kind of leggy. We'll see what it is back in Ohio."

Now Sam returns to digging at what he considers the bottom of the Goliath's burrow. But there's somebody else here, too. "A frog!" Sam cries in surprise as the warty amphibian hops away. The frog has left something behind. At first it looks like a nest of little worms. They turn out to be tadpoles! They were living in a spider burrow and staying moist from their mother's skin.

Sam discovers there are several chambers to the burrow. Who dug it? The frog? Another long-vanished animal? The tarantula herself? That's one of the exciting things about science: Asking questions yields answers, all right, but sometimes it's even more thrilling to discover new questions along the way.

The burrow is an impressive four feet long. "Here's another side chamber," Sam says, now covered with dirt as red as his hair. He keeps on digging with his knife, careful not to hurt the spider by mistake.

Though he's gentle, Sam does seem to be making the tarantula mighty mad. "Now she's kicking!" he announces. "She might be kicking hairs! I'd better get my face out of there."

33

But it's too late. His nose and one of his forearms are burning.

"Here she comes," he announces. He carefully coaxes her out of the burrow. "She's not going to look very nice," he says apologetically. Normally tarantulas spend a great deal of effort keeping themselves clean, almost like cats. They groom by drawing the hairs on their legs through the mouth, using their fangs like the teeth of a comb. Grooming is important, because chemically sensitive hairs on the legs and pedipalps act as taste organs. (Tarantulas are sort of walking on their tongues.) "Those sensitive hairs are no good if they're clotted up with dirt and prey remains," Sam explains. "When a tarantula has a bad hair day," he says, "it's *really* a bad hair day."

Today is a bad day all around for this tarantula. Her hair is a mess. Her burrow's a wreck. And there's no getting away from Sam. He places the open mouth of a plastic Zip-Loc sandwich bag over her, and she is his captive.

But better that Sam should capture her than, say, a coatimundi. This long-snouted relative of the raccoon eats tarantulas when it can manage to bite the spider to death before getting "haired." Sam wants only to weigh and measure her. When you're investigating the life of a little-known animal such as a Goliath birdeater tarantula, it's important to answer the simplest of questions: How big do they get? How fast do they grow? And to get the answers, you have to make many measurements of many spiders over many years.

Sam hangs the bag on the spring balance he carries in his backpack: fifty-two grams. He subtracts the twelve-gram weight of the bag to get the weight of the spider. "She's forty

When a New World tarantula (one from the Americas) is threatened, it uses one of its back legs to brush clouds of irritating hairs from its abdomen. These miniature airborne darts can leave a predator itching for weeks.

grams," he announces. (How much is that? You calculate: one gram equals .035 ounce.) "Not very fat," Sam says. "Her abdomen can get quite a bit larger." Hers is perhaps the size of a nickel. But weight is only one measure of how big a tarantula is. One big meal and that could change fast! So Sam takes another measurement as well. He has found that a better measure of growth is the length of a segment of the leg closest to the front of the spider. He measures this while the spider is in the bag: 30.6 millimeters. (How long is that? You calculate: a millimeter equals .04 inch.) He jots down the figures in his field notebook.

Next, Sam wants to make sure he can keep track of this spider, and make sure when he sees her again that it's her—and not some other Goliath birdeater who has moved into her burrow. Using model paint bought at an Ohio Wal-Mart, he gives her a short red stripe along the knee of her fourth leg. She'll shed this marking when she sheds her skin. He makes a note of the marking in his notebook, too.

Now he can return her to the burrow. He was careful to preserve the burrow entrance, though the rest of it is in ruins. He packs the earth back on top of the excavated burrow. At least she will have a solid roof. Then he opens the bag and shakes her out.

Down the hole she runs. She will probably repair it this evening. "Sorry about that," Sam calls to her. "Good luck!"

FACING PAGE: Sam weighs a captive Goliath and then dabs it with an identifying stripe of red paint.

ABOVE RIGHT: Sam takes a nap in his hammock.

Arachnids All Around

From a car driving along an Arizona highway during July or August, you might see a wonderful sight: dozens of big brown tarantulas streaming across the road. These gentle spiders are Mexican blond tarantulas. They're all males. They're on the move searching for females, who are waiting in their burrows in the hard desert soil.

If you're lucky enough to live in the southwestern United States, you might find lots of different tarantulas in the wild. North of the U.S. border with Mexico, about thirty species of tarantula can be found, from central Missouri to northern California.

No tarantulas near your home? Too bad. But there are plenty of other fascinating spiders to watch. You won't have to go far. In an average North American field, there might be anywhere from 10,000 to 2 million spiders, of many different kinds. New York State and New England combined have about 700 species of spiders. Ohio has 600 species. Florida has 900. Scientists haven't even tried to total up the species of spiders in most states. Maybe you'll be the one to do that!

Spiders offer a close-up look at some of nature's most dramatic moments. Without leaving your own backyard—and probably without even leaving your house—you can see an amazing amount of spider action. You can watch a typical spider build a web; catch, paralyze, wrap, and eat its prey; repair and clean its home; and then

In Arizona, male APHONOPELMA tarantulas leave their burrows and wander the desert, looking for females.

dismantle much of the structure — all within a twenty-four-hour period! And if you watch spiders regularly, you might see more: mothers laying, carrying, or guarding eggs, baby spiders growing up. If you're really lucky, you might see a male spider courting a female. (The little spider is almost always the male, and he's usually pretty wary. After mating, some females snack on their suitors.)

Watching spiders isn't dangerous. Spiders won't attack you. Most spiders won't bite people. Even those that do seldom seriously hurt anyone. Scientists estimate perhaps one in a thousand spiders has venom that could hurt you. (Even black widows don't usually kill people.) In the United States, far more people die from allergic reactions to wasp and bee stings than die from spider bites *and* scorpion stings *combined.*

Still, it's best not to handle spiders. So don't pick them up. You might be allergic to a spider bite, just as some people are allergic to peanuts. And besides, most spiders aren't happy about being picked up by monsters like us! It's good to keep spiders happy, because spiders get rid of flies, gnats, and mosquitoes. Spiders eat more insects than birds do.

Early morning and early evening are often the best times to watch spiders. Web-weaving spiders are busy spinning then. The

Dewy mornings are the best time to go web-spotting.

39

The long-legged cellar spider lives in people's basements and closets all over the world.

whole process can be completed in less than an hour. How many different designs can you find? Webs are easier to see if they are between you and the sun and when they are shiny with morning dew.

But night is a good time for spider watching, too. Go out some night with a headlamp like Sam's. Many spiders come out only at night. Among them are the wolf spiders and the wandering spiders, whose eyes reflect light to help them see in the dark. They glow like tiny diamonds in the beam of your headlamp. A whole bunch of tiny lights glittering in one blob, like a piece of costume jewelry, means you've found a female carrying her babies on her back.

Spider watching is fun anywhere, anytime. In the basement you'll find the long-legged cellar spider. It has long, slender legs and makes a rather loose, messy-looking web. When the spider itself is threatened—by a broom, perhaps—it has a special defense: Hanging upside down, it shakes its web so rapidly that both the spider and the web blur and become nearly invisible.

Look for jumping spiders on fences and the sides of buildings. True to their name, they can leap several times their own body length. But the most striking feature of these spiders is their two big front eyes. They seem to be looking at you—and they are. These two front eyes have incredible vision, better than a hawk's. It's fun to watch them hunt. They attack their prey as cats do, stealthily stalking, then leaping to deliver the killing bite.

Sometimes you don't even have to see the spider to find out what it was doing. The so-called spitting spider — a yellow-and-black-spotted animal with a large, humped head — shoots a strand of glue mixed with venom at its prey. When you find the sucked-dry husk of a fly stuck to the ceiling, you can be sure a spitting spider enjoyed the meal.

A jumping spider trails a silk safety line behind it when it leaps.

Expedition to Les Grottes

When Sam leaves the Trésor Réserve at the end of each day, he says goodbye to some tarantulas—and hello to others.

Meet Clarabelle. She's a black-haired beauty who looks as if she's just had a French pedicure. At the ends of her long legs her toes are tipped in pink. She lives just outside Sam's door at the Emerald Jungle Village nature center, where he spends his nights.

Clarabelle is a pinktoe tarantula—one of the very first tarantulas described by Western scientists. The gentle pinktoes were originally tree-dwelling forest tarantulas, but these days they're happy to build their silky retreats in the eaves of houses, in shrubs, and in the tube-like curves of pineapple leaves on plantations, too. Clarabelle lives in the curled leaves of a potted plant that sits on the tile veranda. One of her fellow pinktoes made an appearance during dinner one night, crawling along the wall of the dining room. (She was looking for dinner, too—though eating from quite a different menu!)

Goliath birdeaters might be Sam's favorites, but no arachnid escapes his interest. And happily, in French Guiana, there are all sorts of them everywhere Sam goes. "There are six species of tarantulas just in the few acres of gardens and woods around the nature center. It's amazing!" he says.

The family that owns Emerald Jungle Village—Joep, Marijka, and ten-year-old Bernie Moonen—is happy to host so many beautiful tarantulas on their land. Joep, who was once the director of the national zoo in the neighboring country of Suriname, studies tropical animals and plants. He knows lots of places nearby where Sam can see unusual spiders and spider relatives. One of them is called Les Grottes (say "Lay Grotz"), French for "The Caves."

Unlike Trésor Réserve, the trail to Les Grottes has no sign. But Joep knows just where it is. It's only half an hour's drive from the nature center. Past the welcome center for Trésor Réserve, past Camp Caiman, another place Sam sometimes stays, you stop just short of a noisy sawmill. To reach the caves, you must walk a slippery mile-and-a-half-long trail through the forest, mostly downhill. There's a lot to see along the way.

Clarabelle, the pinktoe tarantula, has caught a katydid. This large insect meal will provide her with enough food to last many days.

Joep points out many of the plants along the trail. "This one is new to science," Joep says in his soft Dutch accent. "The flower is white. It grows only here. So beautiful!" He points next to a vine: "Look," he says, "this liana is young, so flat! But here, an adult one, looks completely different!"

And see, over here: these short, stout bushy plants have swollen nodes on their stems, Joep points out. Look who's inside! Joep breaks open a node with his fingernail. Tiny brown ants live in these hollows. When the plant's leaves are attacked by bugs, deer, or other leaf-munchers, the ants rush out to defend it. It's like having a live-in police squad at your house.

There are so many strange and wonderful plants in this jungle: Flowers that shoot up straight and white, like tall pieces of blackboard chalk. Leaves that look as if they have been chewed up by bugs—until you notice that each is exactly the same shape. Blooms that splay and pout like swollen lips. Flowers too tiny for anyone to see except the little insects that crawl deep inside the plant to pollinate them.

The rainforest is full of weird surprises, like this walking stick.

Quickly a flash of brilliant orange shoots through the green of the forest canopy. What was *that*?! "The cock-of-the-rock!" cries Joep. "We are very lucky today!" The expedition has just caught a fleeting glimpse of one of the most striking birds in the world. About a foot tall, the male is as orange as a traffic cone. On his head he sports a crest of feathers that starts behind the bright red eye and runs in a tall half-circle all the way to the tip of the beak. He looks as if he is wearing a helmet made out of half an orange. The cock-of-the-rock's brownish mate must be nearby. These birds nest in caves—a sign that Les Grottes must be just around the bend.

Indeed they are. But first there's an obstacle to cross. To get to the caves, you have to walk through another cave, one that's open on both ends, like a tunnel. Water drips from the cave ceiling onto the bauxite rocks on the ground, making them very slippery. Good thing there are plenty of rocks and holes on the cave walls.

But maybe holding on to them isn't such a good idea. "I've never seen so many fer-de-lance as I have seen here," Joep says. "Sometimes as many as two in a day. Be very careful!"

Crossing the hundred-yard-long floor of the entry cave is like walking through a mine-field. Carefully Sam, Joep, and company pick their way over the slippery rocks. They're careful not to disturb snakes. And they're always balancing the heavy load of water, camera gear, an unsheathed cooking knife, Sam's hoe, and other scientific equipment.

Finally, through the tunnel, the big cave yawns before them. The shape of the cave's mouth is familiar. It looks exactly like the burrow of a *really* giant Goliath birdeater tarantula!

When someone points this out to Sam, he pretends to look over his shoulder. His blue eyes widen in mock surprise: "And here she comes!" he jokes.

But what Sam and Joep find hidden in a crevice in the wall of the cave is almost as surprising as a make-believe supersize Goliath. It's called a tailless whip scorpion. Yet it's not a scorpion at all. It doesn't even look like one.

Sam has written about these in one of his books. "They are among the weirdest of the

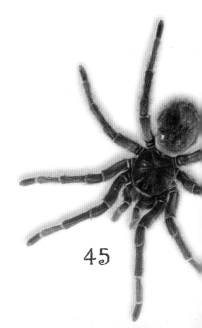

45

FACING PAGE: Tailless whip scorpions thrive inside the cool, dark, moist cave at Les Grottes.

ABOVE: A tailless whip scorpion will carry its young on its back after they hatch.

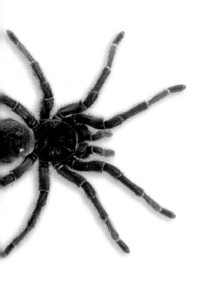

weird," Sam wrote. "They are so strange to behold and observe feeding and moving around that it is a close encounter of the third kind. They are so unearthly in appearance."

The tailless whip scorpion is an arachnid as big as a Goliath birdeater but otherwise very different. It has a flattened body and thin, crazily long legs, several times the length of its body. The longest legs are nearly a foot long. They're right in front of the animal, whipping back and forth. These "whips" give the tailless whip scorpion its name.

Within the arachnids, the tailless whip scorpions belong to an order called Amblypygi ("Am-blee-PIH-jee.") Unlike real scorpions, they have no venom glands, no pincers or stingers. The "whips" are actually a first pair of legs. But they are used not for walking but as sensory organs, like antennae. The tailless whip scorpion moves them around like a blind person using a cane, tapping to feel the way ahead. But imagine having a tool like this: the tailless whip scorpion's "cane" can not only feel, but taste and smell, too!

Seeing the tailless whip scorpion alone would have been worth the trip to Les Grottes. But Sam has another errand to do here. Joep thinks the floor of the cave is a good place for *Holothele* tarantulas. The small, cute tarantulas in this genus are hardly bigger than many species of North American spiders. Sam has been looking for some—but not for himself. They're for one of his students at Hiram College.

Sam knew this student was special the day they met, the first day of the fall semester. Lots of young men and women came to his tarantula lab that day to see if they wanted to work and study there. Students also help out with caring for the spiders—and the food the spiders eat.

"Who wants to clean the cockroach cages?" Sam recalls asking the group.

"Oh, cool!" he heard a girl exclaim as she raised her hand to volunteer.

FACING PAGE: **Sam carefully digs a small HOLOTHELE from its burrow in the cave floor.**

"I knew I had a live one," Sam says.

Now that girl wants to study *Holothele* tarantulas. Amanda Weigand is particularly interested in their love life. She has studied their relatives, called *Heterothele* tarantulas. These tarantulas don't have a prom, but they do dance as they date. The male flutters his legs, jerks his body, taps his feet. And the female, if she's interested, answers his dance with a dance of her own. Amanda wonders if *Holothele* do this, too.

"This is perfect," says Sam, digging into the loose soil on the floor of the cave. It is dotted with little holes and mounds of dirt, like tiny volcanoes—the burrows of the little *Holothele*. Each one contains a young tarantula. "This is like a little nursery for them," Sam explains. "The soil is loose so they can burrow."

One of the little spiders dashes out of its burrow, trying to escape from Sam's waiting pill bottle.

"No, you're not running away!" Sam says to the wiggly tarantula. "You're coming to Ohio!"

At night, Sam catalogues the live tarantula he has collected, ready to take the spider back to his lab in Ohio.

Got Silk?

Spider silk is everywhere. You'll find sheetlike webs in the grass on your lawn. Beautiful orbs hang in windows and on rafters. Funnels of silk appear in barn corners. And (unless someone vacuums much too often) you'll see meshlike webs under the bathroom sink and cobwebs hanging in the basement.

Even though weaving webs is the talent for which spiders are best known, not all spiders do it. But all spiders make silk. It's quite a feat. Spiders make silk from glands inside their abdomens, extruding it through special spigots on their undersides called spinnerets. Some spiders can produce up to seven different kinds of silk, using different spigots on the spinnerets, like a soda fountain, to produce each type.

Spiders don't squirt out their silk. They *pull* it out, using their hind legs, an action that turns the liquid to a solid of amazing strength. A strand of spider silk is stronger than a strand of steel, stronger even than the fabric used for bulletproof vests! And yet spider silk is stretchy, too — it can stretch up to three times its length without breaking.

Silk is such useful material that sometimes birds steal some for their nests. And people use spider silk, too. Warren Knight Instrument Company in Philadelphia keeps two black widow spiders "on the payroll" to make crosshairs for telescopes, optical instruments, and gun sights.

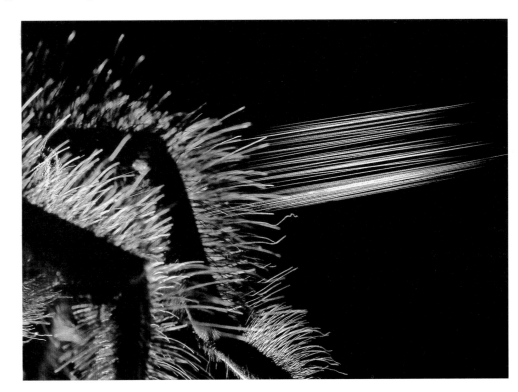

Dozens of fine silk threads emerge from a tarantula's spinnerets. Each strand streams out as a liquid and turns solid in air.

51

(Each spider spins about four feet of silk a day. The people get them to do it by tickling the spiders' bellies with a long straw.)

But it's the spiders themselves, of course, who put silk to best use. It's handy stuff. All spiders need silk to make soft, waterproof cases for their eggs. Many construct silken nurseries for their just-hatched babies. Some spiders catch prey by hurling their silk like a spitball on a thread rather than weaving a web. Lots of spiders hide in silk-lined tunnels, and many of them make trap doors for their burrows, sort of like manhole covers made of silk. Other spiders, including tarantulas, build a special silken "dressing room floor" onto which they shed their skin.

Male spiders have another surprising use for silk. A male spider produces sperm in his abdomen, but he can't transfer it to the female without first spreading that sperm out on a special web he spins just for this occasion. Then he sucks the sperm up into tubes inside his pedipalps, and uses these to transfer the sperm to the female.

Some baby spiders (called spiderlings) make "balloons" out of silk. You may have seen spiderlings ballooning in the fall: They climb up onto fence posts or branches, let loose some silken threads, and let the wind lift them from their perch to float off to a new home.

This SELENOCOSMIA tarantula has used silk to make a tough, waterproof case for her eggs.

But of course the most familiar use of spider silk is in webs. Just about everyone's favorite web is the one Charlotte wove: the classic orb shape, which looks like the spokes of a wheel overlaid with a spiral. Working with all eight legs and spinning with all six spinnerets, your average garden spider can create this wonderful structure in less than an hour.

In an orb web, the spiral part is the snare. Some spiders lay down drops of glue here, which you can see with a magnifying glass. Others make a kind of natural Velcro by fluffing the silk strand with their tarsi, those claws at the end of their legs. The spider doesn't get stuck in its own web because it has oils on its feet, and it stays on the nonsticky part. Spiders eat the sticky part (it's good, healthy protein) and remake this part of the web each day.

Some spiders want their webs to be nearly invisible. Still other spiders use the web as an active lure: They weave designs into their nets to make them look to pollen-hungry insects like giant flowers. But even though spiders have such effective traps, scientists figure that 80 percent of all insects caught in webs actually get away.

When a tree-dwelling AVICULARIA tarantula molts, it first spins a large silken hammock, suspended inside its retreat. Then it lies back in comfort to shed its old skin. The spider's fangs are as white as walrus tusks after molting, but they soon darken like those on the old skin (AT BOTTOM).

Hairy Mats and Hissing Fits

From the outside, the J. H. Barrow Field Station at Hiram College looks sort of like a barn, only bigger. And like a barn, it's full of animals—but not the animals you might expect.

When you enter, an orphaned starling, Hannibal, whistles and chatters a greeting. The bird is likely to be the first to welcome you—that is, if Wally, Sam's friendly border collie, doesn't get there first, followed by Lucy the corgi, waddling on short legs. As you cross the room you'll walk past black laboratory counters, specimen jars, and terraria full of snakes, lizards, toads, and bugs.

Next you'll come to Sam's office. The small room is jammed with spider posters, spider mobiles, plastic spiders, stuffed spiders, books, files, and a mumbling green mealy parrot from South America named Serge.

There's lots going on here. Hiram students are studying all sorts of things about the natural world, including the plants and animals living on 260 acres of beech and maple forest surrounding this building, at the field station's laboratories. But you'll want to zip past those labs today, because you are headed to a specific destination.

FACING PAGE, NEAR LEFT: Sam and Wally at the office.

FACING PAGE, FAR LEFT: Serge is another of Sam's office companions.

54

You pass through one door, and then another. And when that swings open, you're in another world.

It feels almost like a jungle. A huge humidifier and space heater keep the room warm and moist. The room is lined with counters and shelves. On each of them, all kinds of clear containers seem to be crowded, stacked one atop another, piled two and three deep. Plastic shoeboxes. Food storage bins. Wide-mouth coffee jugs. Terraria. Pill vials. Flour bins. Plastic potato salad containers. Glass salt jars. Plastic candy jars. Some still have labels that say "Laffy Taffy." (Sam remembers the response he got when he asked for these empty containers at the student bookstore: "You want to do WHAT with them?") Now, of course, the candy's gone, replaced by soil and bark or sand, and lots of white filmy threads.

That's when you realize: You're surrounded by about five hundred live tarantulas.

Welcome to the Spider Lab.

"It's the only comparative tarantula lab in the world that's global in reach," Sam says by way of a welcome. There are other labs studying tarantulas, but none have so many different species from so many different countries. Here you'll see Tanzanian chestnut tarantulas from Africa. Martinique pinktoes from the Caribbean. You'll meet handsome, striped Thai tiger tarantulas from Asia, shimmering, iridescent *Avicularia* from South America, and aggressive Cameroon red tarantulas from West Africa. (The species most likely to bite are in wide-mouth coffee jars marked with red pen, "*Use Extreme Caution*" and "Potentially Dangerous!")

There are some spiders here who are not tarantulas. (Among them are about forty wolf spiders that Sam's wife, arachnologist Dr. Maggie Hodge, is studying with her students.) But most of them are tarantulas. Many of them originally lived in Sam's apartment. ("It was a two-bedroom apartment," he explains. "One tarantula bedroom and one person

Iridopelma hirsuta (Pocock)

THE SPIDER LAB

WHAT'S GOING ON IN HERE!?!?!

This lab houses a large research collection of tarantulas from around the world. These spiders are part of a research project into the evolution of diversity in a poorly-understood group of organisms. This research includes studies of the evolutionary relationships of different species of tarantulas (phylogeny) and the evolution of the many different lifestyles tarantulas exhibit (ecology).

RULES FOR VISITORS:

1. The lab is climate-controlled for tropical organisms. Please keep the door closed and turn out the lights when you leave.

2. Do not open or move any containers. Many tarantula species are very fast and aggressive and will bite. Accidently releasing a tarantula could end badly for both you and the spider.

I will be glad to show you the spiders and answer any questions. If I am not here please make an appointment.

Please don't take any unsupervised tours!

Thanks!

Sam Marshall
Director, J. H. Barrow Field Station
phone: 527-2141

Poecilotheria fasciata (Latreille) Sri Lankan ornamental tarantula ♀
Photo & ID by Samuel D. Marshall. Habitat: An arboreal species from the Monsoon forests of Sri Lanka. Thought by many to require high humidity, by others not to require high humidity. A water dish only is sufficient for individuals. Tall cages are preferred by most, with something to climb on and build retreats on or within. hair: None known. Feeding: No special requirements (crickets, grasshoppers, etc.).

Welcome to the Spider Lab.

bedroom.") When Hiram College hired Sam to direct the J. H. Barrow Field Station in 1999, it invited him to move his tarantula collection here. The result is the Spider Lab.

Now the collection includes Goliath birdeaters Sam brought back from previous trips to French Guiana; pinktoe tarantulas like Clarabelle; and in one corner, each in its own separate potato salad container, the baby *Holothele* tarantulas Sam collected for Amanda. (Sam carried them back to Ohio in pill vials in his checked luggage. He had special documents in case anyone wondered why he had live tarantulas in his suitcase.)

The Spider Lab is not just a room housing tarantulas. Besides all those containers, you'll also notice Plexiglas boxes with funny tubes in them. There's a microscope. There's a video camera. All these are used in the behavior experiments Sam and his students do with the tarantulas.

How would you figure out if a tarantula can recognize the silk of its own burrow? One way is to provide each of several tarantulas with an identical tube in which to spin a nest. Then swap the nest tubes around and see how the tarantulas react.

"I want to look at how tarantulas *do* these things, these oddball behaviors," Sam says.

One way to understand animals is to simply watch them—in the wild or in the laboratory. Fortunately, tarantulas almost certainly behave in the laboratory much the way they do in the wild. Unlike big animals like tigers or wolves, who need lots of space, most tarantulas don't mind living in the seemingly cramped quarters of a potato salad container. Most species don't roam widely, Sam explains, and they're happiest in a small area where they feel secure. "Tarantulas just do their thing, whether they're in a plastic container from Wal-Mart or on the side of a tree in South America," he says.

Sam has spent many thousands of hours watching tarantulas—in the wild, in the basement, in the laboratory. There is nothing he would rather do! And sometimes a tarantula does something so unusual, so mysterious, that questions start going off in his mind like fireworks.

One time that happened after Sam connected two different sets of observations. Many times he had seen his tarantulas spin special silk mats before shedding their exoskeleton. Sam has always loved to watch his tarantulas do this—though it sometimes makes him a bit anxious, because this is a crucial process for the spider. It's important that nothing go wrong while the new exoskeleton is hardening.

Sam noticed that Goliath birdeaters take an extra step before molting. Right before turning upside down to molt, the spider brushes hairs off the sides and end of its abdomen. The silk mat, then, is covered with light brown hair.

Why would you want to shed your skin on a mat covered with hair?

Sam suspected that the tarantulas had a good reason. And then he remembered something he'd noticed when he had first started collecting Goliath birdeaters in French Guiana: They sometimes had small gray flies on their bodies. The baby flies, or larvae, are like tiny worms, and these sometimes crawl around the base of the spiders' legs, feeding on their blood. They must feel to the spider like fleas to a dog. Yuk!

Happily, shedding your skin helps you get rid of all those parasites. Unless, of course, they can just crawl back on while your new exoskeleton is hardening. You're probably thinking just what Sam was thinking at the time: What might prevent those nasty flies from reinfesting the freshly shed tarantula? Was this why the Goliaths shed hair onto their molting mats?

So Sam conducted a few more experiments. He placed fly larvae on two types of silk mats, one hairy, one not. What happened? You guessed it: On the hairy mats, the larvae quickly became entangled in the long, barbed hairs among the silk strands.

And yet another discovery was made after Sam was watching a wild Goliath birdeater in the field. Sam was eye to eye with a tarantula who was trying to persuade him to retreat. The spider reared up, waved its front legs, extended its fangs, and kicked off hairs. But it was also doing something else. The spider was making a scrubbing motion with its pedipalps and its first and second pairs of legs. Much later, another spider scientist Sam was working with saw the same thing—and, at the same time, heard a remarkable sound coming from the tarantula's cage. The spider, it seemed, was hissing like a cat!

Very few spiders make any sound at all. They don't have vocal cords as we do. They don't have rattles like rattlesnakes. The spider didn't seem to be expelling air through its mouth. Where could the sound be coming from?

Maybe you have the same thought the scientists had: Perhaps the hissing sound had something to do with the strange scrubbing motion. Could it be possible? How to find out?

First, Sam prodded the Goliaths gently with a blunt probe. It didn't hurt the spiders, but it did make them hiss. And when they hissed, Sam recorded the sounds, to analyze them. Sometimes they got really loud—loud enough to be heard from several yards away. But how were they doing it?

Sam came up with an idea, or hypothesis: Perhaps the hissing had something to do with the hairs on the tarantula's front legs. He had looked very carefully at the shed exoskeletons of Goliath birdeaters and noticed something unusual: The pedipalps and first two pairs of legs seemed to have special hairs on them. Some hairs were long and stiff. Others looked bushy, like a bottlebrush. Could they be used to produce sound?

Next came the experiment. If the spiders were using these special hairs to make their warning hiss, there was one way to find out: Shave the spiders' legs.

Even though the hairs would regrow the next time the spiders shed their skins, Sam guessed that the tarantulas wouldn't like the shaving one bit. So he put them to sleep with carbon dioxide first. Then he carefully scraped the hairs from the front legs with a tiny scalpel. After the spiders woke up, he tried provoking them again with that blunt probe. The tarantulas reared up, showed their fangs, struck with their front legs—but couldn't hiss! Shaving their legs had silenced the display.

Molted tarantula skins.

But how can hair make noise? Sam examined the hairs on the legs shed from an exoskeleton under a special electron microscope. The exoskeleton was sprayed with gold to reflect the radiation from the microscope's electron beam. The image, greatly magnified, could be viewed on a computer screen. On it, Sam saw the different types of hair in great detail. The brushlike hairs were more complicated than he thought. Now that they were so greatly magnified, he could see that each hair had a toothed area at the end.

Time for another experiment. Out came the tarantula razor again. But this time, Sam tried shaving off only one hair type per spider. In some spiders, he shaved off only the spiny hairs. In others, he shaved off only the brushy ones. And that's the way he discovered how the sound is produced: This tarantula hisses by combing the teeth on the hairs of one leg through the brushes on the hairs of the opposite leg. The toothed edges of the brushy hairs work and sound just like opening Velcro.

The Goliath birdeater tarantula, Sam discovered, produces sound in a manner unknown in any other living creature. And in making this discovery, he proved—once again—that these primitive "spider dinosaurs" are actually far more sophisticated than anyone had thought.

Images from a scanning electron microscope allowed Sam to see details of the sound-making hairs of a Goliath birdeater.

63

Tarantula Frontiers

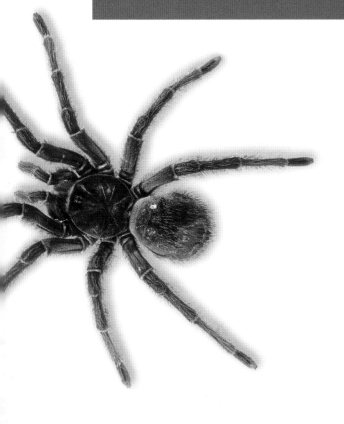

Michelle Hawk is making a film. The stars just happen to be spiders.

The movie isn't a new version of *Arachnophobia*. In the Spider Lab, this Hiram College sophomore has set up a video camera to record the results of her experiment.

Michelle is working with spiders in the family Barychelidae ("beary-CHELL-eh-day.") They're closely related to tarantulas, but somewhat smaller and less hairy. "Very little is known about them," explains Michelle. In fact, when she first tried to read up on this group of spiders before she began her experiments, the only information she could find was that they were "very aggressive."

Hmmm, she thought. "What if they bite me?" she asked her professor.

"You'll be the first to find out!" Sam cheerfully replied.

In fact, this is just what she's working on right now. How aggressive *are* they? Her experiment will record how the spiders respond to being prodded with a slender, foot-long tube.

As the camera rolls, the student pokes the long glass tube at the first spider. It wisely runs away. Same with the second spider. In fact, all these "aggressive" spiders just seem

Michelle studies the aggressive response of her study spider in Sam's lab.
Almost five hundred live tarantulas are housed in containers around her.

to want to get away from this thing—until one spider turns the tables. It rears up and bites the giant tube!

"AHHHH!" Michelle cries in surprise. And in the excitement, she accidentally flicks the tube—and sends the spider flying.

"The spider's loose! The spider's loose!" Michelle calls out in alarm. Five other students in the lab scramble to rescue the spider. The video records the bedlam. Eventually, one student throws a cup over the escapee. The spider is then returned to its potato salad container to recover from the ordeal.

This was just the sort of thing Michelle's mother worried about when she and her daughter first visited Hiram as they were looking at colleges. When they toured the Spider Lab, they saw a bunch of shed tarantula exoskeletons piled in a shoebox. It looked to them as if these skins were live tarantulas—loose. Both women screamed.

"Most people don't know anything about spiders because they're afraid of them," Michelle now explains to visitors, with the calm of a mature scientist. "I was a little nervous working with them at first. But it's not like I was going to squish them." Now Michelle is wrapped up in the excitement of science. "Basically," she says, "everything I find out about spiders is fascinating."

Sam's students are at the frontiers of spider science. "You have to watch them," Sam promises the students at the Spider Lab. "You just have to wait a number of hours to have some secret revealed. You never know when you'll see something so cool that the other ninety-nine hours of watching nothing is worth it."

Following in their professor's footsteps, these students are investigating some of the most basic—and therefore most important—questions about how these giant, ancient spiders live.

Two of Sam's students documented a rare event among spiders: sharing food. Many animals seem quite selfish when it comes to food. Even a nice dog will sometimes growl if you approach the food dish while he's eating. And spiders are so focused on food that females sometimes eat their boyfriends!

But dining etiquette that would please even Miss Manners is not rare among West African Cameroon red tarantulas—at least among brothers and sisters. And the first people to scientifically document them were Sam's students.

Melissa Varrecchia and Vanessa Gorley fed frozen crickets to groups of baby brother and sister tarantulas. With most spiders, you might expect that they would all grab for the food at once—or even try to eat each other. But instead, to the students' astonishment, the young spiders fed from the same cricket without fighting. Often they even ate side by side—sometimes with legs interlocked, almost as if they were holding hands!

Actually, tarantulas can be downright gentlemanly and ladylike. That's the conclusion Amanda Weigand came to

Two Goliath birdeater tarantulas about to mate. This is a very dangerous time for a male (he is at bottom right, facing the female at top left). He has to reach underneath the female's huge fangs to place his pedipalps in a small pocket under her body. Luckily for him, female Goliaths rarely attack their dates, unlike some other tarantulas.

when she was studying the East African tarantula *Heterothele villosela* and made her own exciting discoveries.

Amanda wants to be a marine mammal trainer one day. But there are few whales in Ohio. Amanda thought she could start small, by working with spiders. Sam suggested she look into spider dating. No one had ever recorded the mating behavior of *Heterothele villosela* before.

So Amanda soon found herself playing matchmaker to tarantulas.

Amanda dropped a male into a female's container. "That's when he would start to court her," Amanda explains. "The male uses his first left leg and his first right leg to drum once, or twice, by twitching in front of her, with his two legs touching her web. He would twitch on the web until she responded. What a gentleman, don't you think?"

Yes, indeed!

The male tarantula is not touching the web just to tug at her heartstrings. Remember that spiders can smell and taste with their feet. Female spiders secrete a chemical signal in their silk to let males know when they are looking for a mate.

Amanda found that the interested female answers the male's dance with one of her own. She fans her right and left front legs alternately up and down. Slowly, carefully, the dancing pair come closer together. The male extends a leg to touch one of hers. The male raises the female up, reaches

Amanda uses a video camera to record the parental care of her study spider, HETEROTHELE VILLOSELA, housed in a plastic container.

beneath her with his sperm-containing pedipalps, and mates with her.

Then the male runs for his life. The romance is over.

"One time she ripped off his leg," Amanda recounts. "In another species, the female fanged the male and I could hear it crunch. It was gross!"

In the end, ten of Amanda's pairs courted and mated. Two months later, sixty tick-size baby tarantulas hatched out of an egg sac. And with them, a new opportunity for discovery.

Eager to feed the new babies, Amanda plucked two large crickets out of the food terrarium and gave them to the mother and young.

She was amazed: The female grabbed one large cricket in her fangs. Some of the babies clustered around the mother's mouth. Around the other cricket, the babies gathered, sharing the food—just the way the tarantulas from the opposite side of the African continent did!

This is one reason she wanted those *Holothele* that Sam brought back from Les Grottes. They are a similar kind of tarantula. They are all babies now, but they'll grow up soon. Amanda wants to investigate their courtship and child rearing. Do these tarantulas also have a courtship dance?

She'll be the first to find out.

"Elle Est Belle, le Monstre"

Back at Trésor Réserve in French Guiana, nine children from the little village of Roura gather by the head of the jungle trail. They all go to school with Joep and Marijke's son, Bernie. They are on a special expedition today. They're going to meet the Tarantula Scientist!

Joep begins to introduce Sam to the children in French: *"On voit aujourd'hui Dr. Marshall . . ."* ("We see today Dr. Marshall . . .")

But Sam would rather introduce them to someone else.

"Let's show them Clarabelle!" he suggests.

Off comes the plastic lid of the deli carton he pulls from his backpack. Slowly, a big, black, hairy leg arcs over the lip of the container—and then another leg, and another. Clarabelle steps right into Sam's hand. "Here she comes!" Sam says to the students.

"Does anyone want to hold her?" Sam asks Bernie and Joep to translate.

"Qui veut la toucher?" ("Who wants to touch her?") says Bernie. And there is a moment of silence.

Then one little hand shoots out—a ten-year-old boy in a gray baseball cap and a Reebok

T-shirt. The pinktoe tarantula steps carefully from Sam's open palm to the boy's. Then another child reaches out, and another. Finally, nine palms stretch out to hold the spider. Even the ten-year-old girl with four short braids who said earlier that day that she was afraid of spiders. Even the little boy wearing a Spiderman T-shirt who's only six years old.

Now Bernie tells his schoolmates there's another kind of tarantula Sam can show them. It lives in a hole off the trail. Who wants to go see it?

"*Moi! Moi!*" ("Me! Me!") every child cries enthusiastically. So the group follows Sam to a hole where a Goliath bird-eater is living. Everyone sits in silence while Sam twizzles the giant spider out of the hole.

"*Voilà!*" says Sam, as the big female Goliath rushes out of the burrow. "Wow, she's a beauty!"

The giant tarantula stays outside the hole for perhaps five seconds. All the onlookers hold their breath. The spider realizes that there is no insect prey and that she is surrounded by probing eyes. She darts back down the hole.

Only then does one of the children dare speak. A little girl murmurs in awe, almost under her breath: "*Elle est belle, le monstre.*" ("She is beautiful, the monster.")

* * *

Sam is happy to spend his life studying these beautiful monsters. Like his students, he's thrilled to be on the cutting edge of scientific discovery, finding out new things about fascinating creatures.

But for Sam, just learning about them is not enough. He also wants to give something back.

Do tarantulas need people to help them? To find out, all you have to do is visit any souvenir shop in French Guiana's capital city, Cayenne. There, on the shelves among the postcards and T-shirts, you'll see one of the most popular tourist items: dead Golaith birdeater tarantulas, framed behind glass or encased in plastic.

These curios may look cool at first. After all, this is one huge, beautiful spider. But each one of these animals was alive, living as vividly as a jaguar among the leaf litter of the rainforest. Each of these giant spiders was enjoying her otherworldly, sensitive, spidery life—until someone killed her for a tourist's souvenir.

The school kids discover, with careful respect, how a pinktoe tarantula can be handled.

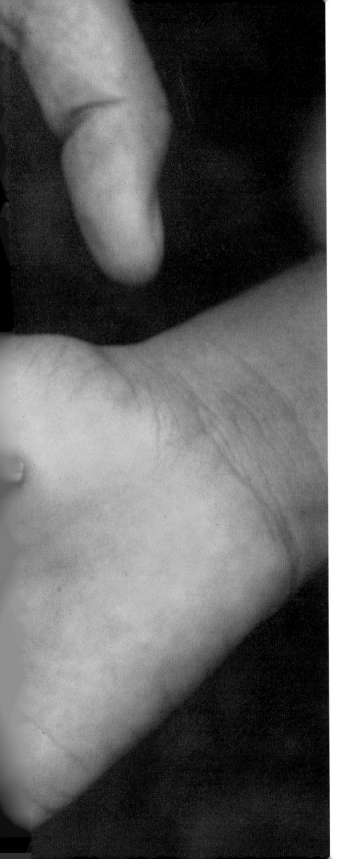

No one knows for sure how many tarantulas are killed for this trade. Sam estimates it must be many thousands. There is no limit to the number of Goliath birdeater tarantulas you can legally kill in French Guiana. "How much can they take," Sam worries, "and still survive as a species?"

This is one reason Sam is conducting his population studies. He wants to find out if too many Goliaths are dying and, if so, provide the data the French government needs to make laws to protect these spiders.

And this is one reason Sam wanted to let the children of Roura meet wild tarantulas. This is why Sam loves to teach older students at Hiram's Spider Lab. "We need young people to learn to care about tarantulas," he says, "and to make sure there's always a place for tarantulas in the world."

Why do we need tarantulas on our planet? There are lots of reasons. For one, a tarantula might one day save your life.

Chilean tarantula venom might help heart attack victims. Researchers at the University of Buffalo in New York have found a protein in its venom that might help block fibrillation, the rapid, uncoordinated twitching of the heart muscle that is a major cause of death after heart attacks. Another protein in the same species' venom might stop the growth of brain tumors. Scientists are also studying a substance in Cameroon red tarantulas' venom. They hope it could lead to a new class of medicines for the treatment of nerve problems.

Tarantulas have a lot to teach us. For 150 million years, tarantulas have evolved and adapted. "Because they're so old, they have a lot to show us about the history of the planet," Sam says. "What was it like on that ancient supercontinent, Gondwanaland? And what was

Hands reach out for close contact of the spidery kind.

it like when Gondwanaland split up, when tarantulas traveled the world on drifting continents?"

Sam could go on naming reasons to study tarantulas. He could list even more reasons why we should care about their survival in the wild.

But for the tarantula scientist, it all boils down to this:

"It's really just a part of something awesome," Sam says. "To see this spider, and see how it lives—there's nothing quite like it. It's a jewel in a beautiful setting, down here in this forest.

"These giant tarantulas are a sign of a healthy Amazonian rainforest environment," he continues. "It's an integral part of an ecosystem."

Would the whole jungle fall apart if one tarantula species went extinct? No one knows. But one thing's for sure. Without these awesome, regal spiders, the jungle—and our world—would be a lonelier, smaller, less exciting, and less mysterious place.

Sam understands the fascination people have for tarantulas. But it makes him sad to see these wonderful spiders killed and sold as tourist trinkets.

As of this printing, the Spider Lab at Hiram College is closed and Sam is doing research on tarantulas and other spiders at the University of Cincinnati, where he began his tarantula studies. Look for him on the Wed!

Tarantulas Prefer Not to Be Handled

Unless you are working with an expert like Sam, or become one yourself, you really shouldn't handle tarantulas. It makes them scared, and they might bite or leave their irritating hairs on you. And remember, though tarantula venom isn't deadly, some people have allergic reactions to spider venom (just as some people have allergic reactions to bee stings). Some people react very badly to tarantula hair (just as some react badly to poison ivy). The safest thing for both you and the tarantula? Observe the spider carefully from a respectful distance.

Spider Stats

A few surprising numbers about spiders . . .

Spider species named so far by scientists: 37,000

Spider species scientists think there really are: 70,000 to 170,000

Tarantula species so far recorded: about 850

Tarantula species in the United States: about 30

Leg span, in inches, of the largest spider on Earth, the Goliath birdeater tarantula: 12

Individual spiders in an average American field: 10,000 to 2 million

Amount of silk a golden orb weaver can potentially spin in a minute, in feet: 6

Spiders you need to make a pound of silk from egg sacs: 663,522

Different kinds of silk a single spider might be able to make: 7

Years a tarantula might live in captivity: 30

Record number of years a tarantula has gone without food: 2

Relative humidity required by most tropical tarantulas: 70 to 80 percent

Relative humidity in average American home: 15 percent

Relative toxicity of black widow venom, compared with equal volume of rattlesnake venom: 15 to 20 times more toxic

Chances that any given spider might bite and hurt you: 1 in 1,000

Chemically sensitive hairs on the body of an adult spider: over 1,000

Millions of years tarantulas have existed on Earth: more than 150

In self-defense, this Mexican redknee tarantula has kicked off a blizzard of tiny dartlike hairs from its abdomen. These will stick painfully in the skin, eyes, and nose of any attacker.

Spider Speak

Like all scientists, arachnologists have a special technical language all their own for talking about spiders and spider relatives. You won't need a decoder ring if you already know these terms:

Arachnids: spiders and their eight-legged relatives.

Arachnologist: a scientist who studies arachnids.

Arachnophile: a person who appreciates arachnids.

Arachnophobe: a person who unreasonably fears arachnids, especially spiders.

Book lungs: the old-fashioned breathing organs of spiders, which resemble a stack of papers or the pages of a book. Book lungs are the only breathing organs that tarantulas have.

Ballooning: the way spiders use silk to ride the wind to a new location. Baby spiders often use this method to leave the nest.

Cephalothorax: the spider's head, containing (among other things) the sucking stomach.

Chelicerae: the spider's two-part jaw, the last segment of which ends in a fang.

Cuticle: the strong, light, waterproof material that composes the external skeletons of invertebrates from shrimp to spiders—and even the hairs on tarantulas.

Cymbium: the bulblike structure on the last joint of the pedipalps in male spiders, which he uses to transfer his sperm to the female spider.

Egg sac: the silken purse the mother spider weaves to hold her eggs. Sometimes she carries this around in her mouth.

Exoskeleton: the external skeleton of invertebrates.

Hairy mygalomorphs: another name for tropical tarantulas (as opposed to the Mediterranean wolf spider who inspired the tarantella dance of Italy).

Hemolymph: spider blood, which is never red, but might be clear or light blue.

Invertebrates: the more than 90 percent of animals on Earth who don't have internal skeletons.

Pedipalps: the food-handling legs (or arms, depending on your point of view) at the front of the spider's head. The male also uses these to transfer sperm to the female.

Slit sensillae: the sense organs on spiders' legs that permit them to tell, from very faint vibrations, the size of an approaching critter, be it a cricket in the leaf litter or a person entering the door of the laboratory across the room.

Spiderlings: baby spiders, often quite different in color from the adults.

Spinnerets: the nozzlelike dispensers of spider silk on the back of the abdomen.

Stridulation: the act of making sound by rubbing one body part against another. Singing crickets produce their chirps by stridulating with their wings. Goliath birdeater tarantulas stridulate with hairs near their mouths, producing a warning hiss.

Tarsi: the two claws at the end of spiders' walking feet.

Tracheae: breathing tubes that lead from the outside of the spider deep into the body. Most modern spiders have them, but not tarantulas.

Theraphosidae: the spider family to which tarantulas belong.

How This Book Was Researched

Author Sy Montgomery and photographer Nic Bishop accompanied Sam Marshall on an expedition to French Guiana in South America. We stayed with him at the Moonen family's wonderful Emerald Jungle Village nature center. With Sam, we searched out tarantula burrows and marked and measured tarantulas in Trésor Réserve. We accompanied Sam and Joep to Les Grottes, where we glimpsed the cock-of-the-rock, met the tailless whip scorpions, and collected *Holothele* tarantulas. We enjoyed meeting the children at Bernie's school as we learned together how to handle the patient and gentle Clarabelle.

We also visited Sam's Spider Lab at Hiram College in Hiram, Ohio, where he was an assistant professor of biology. There we enjoyed meeting Sam's students, including Michelle Hawk and Amanda Weigand; Sam's wife, arachnologist Dr. Maggie Hodge; two of their dogs; one of their parrots; several of their colleagues; and hundreds of their spiders. We learned from them all. To everyone who helped us—grownups and children, North and South Americans, scientists, students, and spiders—we extend our heartfelt thanks.

Special Acknowledgments

Besides our vertebrate and invertebrate subjects, we would like to thank some of the people who helped us behind the scenes. We are grateful to Jim Crisman of Crisman Communications Consulting for putting us in touch with Sam in the first place; Bob Oksner, for his helpful criticisms of the manuscript; Dr. Gary Galbreath, for evolutionary assistance; our wonderful editor, Amy Flynn, at Houghton Mifflin, for her vision and encouragement; and Kate O'Sullivan, who oversaw this book in its final stages.

Joep, Sam, Sy, and the children of l'Ecole Augustine Duchange Elementary School at the Trésor Réserve.

Selected Bibliography

In addition to what we learned on our travels, these books were helpful in researching our story, and we thought you might like them, too.

Tarantulas and Other Arachnids by Sam Marshall (Hauppauge, N.Y.: Barron's Educational Services, 2001). Marketed as a pet owner's manual, it's that and much more. Written by the star of this book, *Tarantulas and Other Arachnids* is fun and fact-packed, whether you hope to meet tarantulas in the wild or in captivity. You'll love the great photos!

Spiders and Their Kin by Herbert W. Levi and Lorna R. Levi (New York: Golden Press, 1990.) This helpful, easy-to-use, 160-page guidebook is great for helping both kids and adults identify spiders in their neighborhoods and learn about others around the world. Its small size makes it easy to carry with you.

Florida's Fabulous Spiders by Sam Marshall and G. B. Edwards (Tampa, Fla.: World Publications, 2001). Sam and a fellow arachnologist team up to bring you a delightful collection of spider pictures, poetry, history, facts, and lore, along with descriptions of many of Florida's nine hundred spider species. Both kids and adults will enjoy it.

Spiders on the Web

American Tarantula Society: www.atshq.org/index.shtml. People who own, study, and admire tarantulas discuss their favorite spiders and how to study, protect, and raise them.

American Arachnological Society: http://americanarachnology.org/. Professional arachnologists as well as amateurs present new information about spiders and their relatives. The society's members meet once a year.

International Society of Arachnology: http://arachnology.org/. A round-the-world organization of arachnophiles that holds meetings once every three years.

If You Visit French Guiana

Emerald Jungle Village, where Sam bases his tarantula expeditions, has special programs for families with kids. You can write to

Emerald Jungle Village
Carrefour du Gallion
97356 Montsinery (Guyane)
France

(That's right—France. French Guiana is technically part of France, even though it's not physically attached—the same way that Puerto Rico is part of the United States.)

Or you can send an e-mail to emeraldjunglevillage@wanadoo.fr.

If You Buy a Tarantula

You can probably buy a tarantula at your local pet store. But read Sam's book about them first. Sadly, some pet stores don't know how to keep a tarantula healthy in captivity. They might even sell you a sick spider. As a result, many tarantulas suffer and die. Before you get one, learn how to recognize a healthy spider and how to keep it happy.

Some tarantulas are becoming rare because too many are taken from the wild. Before you buy one, find out where your tarantula really came from. One way to know for sure is to order from a company that specializes in baby tarantulas that were bred in captivity.

Index